DISCARD

HEROES OF
RACING

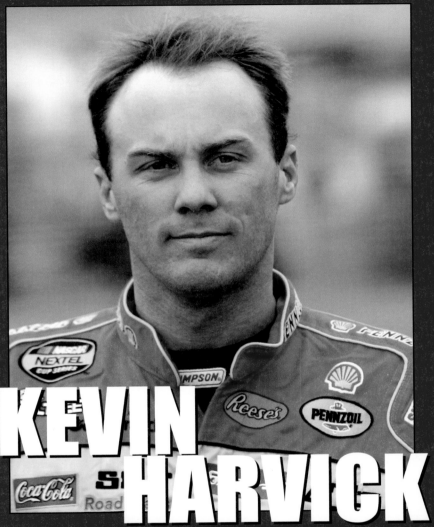

KEVIN
HARVICK

Racing to the Top

by Tom Robinson

Enslow Publishers, Inc.

40 Industrial Road
Box 398
Berkeley Heights, NJ 07922
USA
http://www.enslow.com

Library of Congress Cataloging-in-Publication Data
Robinson, Tom.
  Kevin Harvick : racing to the top / Tom Robinson.
    p. cm. — (Heroes of racing)
  Summary: "A biography of American NASCAR driver Kevin Harvick"—Provided by publisher.
  Includes bibliographical references and index.
  ISBN-13: 978-0-7660-3299-6
  ISBN-10: 0-7660-3299-X
  1. Harvick, Kevin—Juvenile literature. 2. Automobile racing drivers—United States—Biography—Juvenile literature. I. Title.
  GV1032.H357R63 2009
  796.72092—dc22
  [B]
                                            2008007697

Printed in the United States of America

10 9 8 7 6 5 4 3 2 1

To Our Readers: We have done our best to make sure all Internet addresses in this book were active and appropriate when we went to press. However, the author and the publisher have no control over and assume no liability for the material available on those Internet sites or on other Web sites they may link to. Any comments or suggestions can be sent by e-mail to comments@enslow.com or to the address on the back cover.

Disclaimer: This publication is not affiliated with, endorsed by, or sponsored by NASCAR. NASCAR®, WINSTON CUP®, SPRINT CUP, NATIONWIDE SERIES, NEXTEL CUP, BUSCH SERIES and CRAFTSMAN TRUCK SERIES are trademarks owned or controlled by the National Association for Stock Car Auto Racing, Inc., and are registered where indicated.

♻ Enslow Publishers, Inc. is committed to printing our books on recycled paper. The paper in every book contains 10% to 30% post-consumer waste (PCW). The cover board on the outside of each book contains 100% PCW. Our goal is to do our part to help young people and the environment too!

Photo credits: Jason Babyak/AP Images, 1; Ric Feld/AP Images, 4; David Graham/AP Images, 10, 97; James Yee/AP Images, 15; Bob Brodbeck/AP Images, 18; Roy Dabner/AP Images, 22; David Duprey/AP Images, 27; Tony Gutierrez/AP Images, 31; Matt Slocum/AP Images, 35; Nam Y. Huh/AP Images, 37; Jim Topper/AP Images, 40; Alan Marler/AP Images, 46; Donna McWilliam/AP Images, 49; Skip Stewart/AP Images, 57; Scott Trigg/AP Images, 65; Phil Manson/AP Images, 66; Terry Renna/AP Images, 70; Seth Rossman/AP Images, 76; Glenn Smith/AP Images, 81, 105; Russ Hamilton/AP Images, 86; Wayne Scarberry/AP Images, 91; John Raoux/AP Images, 108

Cover Photo: Jason Babyak/AP Images

CONTENTS

REPLACING A LEGEND

The world of NASCAR racing had hardly even begun its most difficult healing process when Kevin Harvick stepped out of the darkness and into the spotlight.

On February 21, 2001—the day that Dale Earnhardt was being buried in a private ceremony—race team owner Richard Childress introduced Harvick as Earnhardt's replacement during a press conference in Rockingham, North Carolina. "We're going to do what Dale would want us to do, and that's race," Childress said.[1]

Kevin Harvick and his crew celebrate after winning the NASCAR Cracker Barrel Old Country Store 500 in 2001.

The status as Earnhardt's replacement was in many ways a technicality. Harvick knew that no one was expecting him or anyone else to be able to actually replace one of stock car racing's all-time legendary figures. Harvick did, however, take Earnhardt's spot on the Richard Childress Racing team and thus was in position to answer the questions the team faced during its mourning.

"Dale Earnhardt was probably the best race car driver there ever is going to be in NASCAR and nobody will ever replace him," Harvick said at the press conference that day. "And, I think we all know that. So, I would hope that you guys don't expect me to replace him because nobody ever will."[2]

RACING TRAGEDY

Dale Earnhardt was only about a half-mile (0.8 kilometers) from finishing the 2001 Daytona 500. He did not have a chance to win, but was still battling for fourth place when his car grazed Sterling Marlin's, sending Earnhardt's car straight into the wall at about 180 miles (289.68 kilometers) per hour before being struck by Ken Schrader's car.

NASCAR officials have had frequent discussions, before and after the crash, about how to best balance keeping their sport safe while maintaining the excitement of high-speed racing. On that day, the blunt-force trauma to Earnhardt's head from the straight-on hit to the wall was too much. He died instantly at the age of forty-nine.

"This is undoubtedly one of the toughest announcements I have ever personally had to make," NASCAR president Mike Helton said as he prepared to break the news to the public. "We've lost Dale Earnhardt."[3] NASCAR chairman Bill France Jr. said, "NASCAR has lost its greatest driver ever, and I personally have lost a great friend."[4]

SPEEDING UP THE PLAN

Harvick's biggest career break came as a result of one of the saddest events in the thrilling and sometimes dangerous sport's history. Earnhardt's death accelerated a process that was in the works. Harvick had already shown that he was a driver capable of a spot competing on the highest level of NASCAR, but he was now in that position sooner than he had anticipated.

Childress explained that he had plans for Harvick to run between five

KEVIN HARVICK

Date of Birth:
December 8, 1975

Hometown:
Bakersfield, California

Wife: DeLana

Pets: 3 dogs, 2 cats

NASCAR debut: 2001

and seven NASCAR Winston Cup races in 2001 and move into a full-time spot in 2002. Instead, he was now being placed in the GM Goodwrench car with the No. 29, instead of Earnhardt's famous number 3, just one race into the 2001 season. "This happened a lot sooner than any of us ever expected, and it isn't the way Kevin wanted to get into a Winston Cup car," Childress said.[5]

As teammates, Earnhardt had been advising Harvick and also had expected to be racing with him. "I've got all the confidence in the world, and Dale had a lot of confidence in Kevin Harvick's driving ability," Childress said.[6]

That confidence, which Earnhardt had expressed to Harvick in talks inside their trailer at race sites, gave Harvick hope that he was ready to handle the challenge.

"I think this is what Dale Earnhardt would want to happen," Harvick said. "It will be tough, but we're a pretty tough team and we're going to do the best we can. Hopefully, there'll be that one time when you can get out of the car and say, 'that one was for Dale,' when we win our first race."[7]

DID YOU KNOW?

Dale Earnhardt entered the 2001 season as NASCAR's active leader in career victories with 76.

FIRST VICTORY

Harvick did not need long to live out the dream of winning a race for Earnhardt. Less than a month and just three races after Earnhardt's death, Harvick was already taking a victory lap at the Cracker Barrel Old Country Store 500 at Atlanta Motor Speedway. Childress looked on with tears in his eyes as Harvick reached his hand out the window and raised three fingers in salute of racing's famous No. 3.

> **FAST START**
> Kevin Harvick was just the fifth driver—and first since 1963—to win a NASCAR Cup race in his third career start. The others were Bob Flock in 1949, Johnny Mantz in 1950, Bill Norton in 1951, and Dan Gurney in 1963.

The day was full of tributes for Earnhardt. On the third lap of the race, it was the fans who were holding up three fingers as they stood when 7,000 black balloons were released by track officials in memory of Earnhardt. The third lap salute became a part of NASCAR races around the country in 2001.

Harvick had to work for the win. Jeff Gordon, who had already won three of his four season titles at that point, charged underneath coming out of the

CLOSEST RACES IN NASCAR HISTORY
(since the beginning of electronic timing in 1993)

First — Ricky Craven over Kurt Busch, Darlington, 2003, .002 seconds

Second (tie) — Jamie McMurray over Kyle Busch, Daytona (July race), 2007, .005

Second (tie) — Dale Earnhardt over Ernie Irvan, Talladega (July race), 1993, .005

Fourth — Kevin Harvick over Jeff Gordon, Atlanta, 2001, .006 seconds

final turn and was gaining ground as the finish line approached. Gordon had the speed to get past Harvick, but he ran out of time. Harvick was still in front, by less than a foot, when the cars passed the finish line, giving the rookie the victory in just his third start.

"The circumstances that we won the first race under . . . we won't ever forget that moment just because of everything that went on," Harvick said in a 2007 interview. "When I start thinking about it, it brings those same chills back that I got at that

Fans raise three fingers in salute of Dale Earnhardt, Sr.

THEY SAID IT

"What Kevin did for us in 2001, I'll never be able to thank him for it."

— Richard Childress, owner, Richard Childress Racing

particular time of winning my first race. I know that I can't do that again and that's obviously because of the circumstances. Those are the kind of situations as professionals that you dream about. You look for that opportunity to take those moments and try to capitalize on them."[8]

A team that held together during tragedy celebrated as they remembered their star. "It took an extra lap to get the emotional part out of the way," Harvick said. "Then, pulling into Victory Lane and seeing all these guys who put their arms around me and supported me through probably one of the hardest times of their lives—and the hardest situation of my life—was very special."[9]

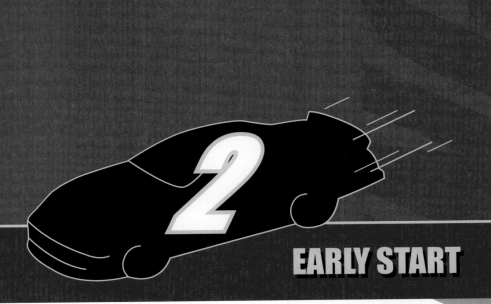

EARLY START

When Kevin Harvick says, "racing is something I've wanted to do my whole life," he is only exaggerating a little.[1] Harvick began learning about cars about the same time he learned how to walk, and he started racing before he started first grade.

As a toddler, Kevin played in a playpen in the garage as Mike Harvick combined watching his son with fixing cars. Kevin liked watching his father work so much that his parents decided to give him a go-kart to celebrate the end of kindergarten.

Kevin made sure the gift was not just a toy and racing was not just a hobby. He raced go-karts for ten years. During that time, he won seven national championships and two grand national championships. "I don't think there's a better way to learn," Kevin said. "You learn car control, weight transfer, how to drive in traffic, how to make the best use of the power you have."[2]

Kevin was a fan of Indy-style, open-wheeled cars and enjoyed watching the Indianapolis 500 on television. When it became time to move up from go-karts, however, Mike had a more practical answer. He built his son's first stock car to begin racing in late model events in Southern California.

THE HARVICK FAMILY

Father: Mike

Mother: JoNell

Sister: Amber

Brother: Clayton

"It was a stock car that paid for his racing," said Mike, who worked as a fireman and ran his own motorsports shop in Bakersfield, California. "We had to work to race. We built stock cars, so that's what we raced."[3]

Harvick kisses the bricks after winning the Brickyard 400.

Kevin's tendency to crash gave him plenty of opportunities to work with his father on getting cars ready to race again. "He started racing here when he was still in school," said Marion Collins, who runs the Mesa Marin Speedway, where Kevin had his first significant stock car win in 1993. "Mike and Kevin worked together on the cars. His dad was with him right up until Kevin started to get offers of rides. Mike's a fantastic chassis man."[4]

ALL IN THE FAMILY

Mike Harvick, Kevin's father, remains active in auto racing. In addition to working on building stock cars in Bakersfield, he serves as a crew chief on the regional level of NASCAR.

Although Kevin dabbled in just about every youth sport available and was a successful wrestler at Bakersfield North High School, the skill and enthusiasm he showed when behind the wheel were leading him to devote more time to racing.

Kevin won the Mesa Marin track championship in his second year there in 1993. While still in high school, he raced part-time in the Featherlite Southwest Series, one of nine NASCAR touring series spread around the country. The Featherlite Southwest Series was Kevin's first exposure to NASCAR racing, giving him the chance to compete against other up-and-coming driving prospects as well as veterans who made a career of racing on that level.

DID YOU KNOW?

NASCAR stands for North American Stock Car Auto Racing.

When he began racing more regularly in the Featherlite Southwest Series, Kevin was named the series' Rookie of the Year in 1995. That year, he won a race in Tucson, Arizona, and finished eleventh in the points standings. "Since I was a little boy, I knew racing was what I wanted to do," Kevin said. "I worked on my career, although it seemed slow at times."[5]

Harvick and his crew celebrate a victory in the NASCAR Busch Series Cabela's 250 in 2003.

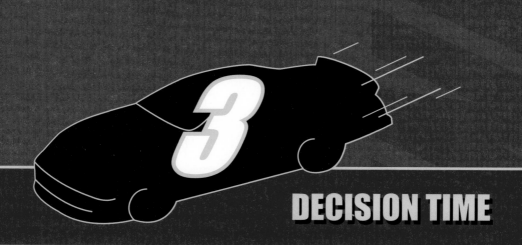

The lower levels of racing can be entertaining, but they are not a way to make a living. Racing at local tracks needs to be either a hobby or a stepping-stone toward a career.

Kevin Harvick reached that realization at twenty-one years old. His driving success was drawing attention and possible chances to move up, but Harvick was also taking classes as a part-time student at Bakersfield Junior College. He could take his studies more seriously and pursue a career in architecture or put more time trying to make driving a career.

Harvick knew it was time to make that decision. "In 1997, when I was attending Bakersfield Junior College, the time came for me to make a choice about my future," Harvick said. "I either had to focus on racing full-time, or decide on a new profession and begin training for it. I chose racing and I've never looked back."[1]

After running one NASCAR Winston West Series race in 1996, Harvick entered three races in 1997 and twice finished in the top ten. The chance to race cars evolved, in part, from racing trucks on the national level.

TRUCK CAREER

Harvick raced once in the NASCAR Craftsman Truck Series in 1995, starting and finishing twenty-seventh in a truck his father owned when the circuit had a race at his local track, Mesa Marin. Harvick made four appearances on the tour in 1996 and made the most of a stop at his home track. After placing thirty-fifth, thirty-first, and thirtieth in his earlier attempts that season and leaving two of the races early after crashing, he had his best performance to date at Mesa Marin. Harvick qualified seventh and finished eleventh.

"We didn't have the money to afford to take him where he wanted to go," Mike Harvick said. "The only way he was going to make a career out of this

Kevin Harvick (rear) edges out Ted Musgrave near the finish line for his first victory in the Craftsman Truck Series.

was to move on to a professional team. I understand that."[2]

With proof that he could compete and more time to devote to racing, Harvick was out racing in the Craftsman Truck Series for half of the 1997 races, appearing in thirteen of twenty-six. Spears Racing offered that chance. "We were going to run a second

NASCAR CRAFTSMAN TRUCK DRIVING CAREER

Year	Races	Wins	Top 5	Poles	Earnings	Rank
1995	1	0	0	0	$1,450	84
1996	4	0	0	0	$14,800	58
1997	13	0	0	0	$82,195	26
1998	26	0	3	0	$244,066	17
1999	25	0	6	0	$322,179	12
2001	1	0	1	0	$24,550	122
2002	5	1	3	0	$89, 055	30
2003	6	1	3	0	$89,760	30
2004	2	0	2	0	$22,150	53
2005	3	0	2	0	$37,030	55
2007	6	0	3	0	$72,425	36
Total	92	2	23	0	$999,550	NA

truck and put him in it," Al Hoffman of Spears said. "We decided that we liked him. We knew he had a lot of talent and he sure could drive."[3]

Driving the trucks took some adjustment and Harvick never stopped racing cars. "Once he got comfortable, he was a serious contender," Hoffman said. "Having Kevin around made everyone want to work for him."[4]

Spears Racing and Harvick were both trying to establish themselves. "I think Kevin was better than this equipment," said Greg Biffle, who raced against him then and throughout his climb through the NASCAR ranks. "I think it was a case that he didn't

NASCAR CRAFTSMAN TRUCK SERIES

NASCAR ventured into truck racing in 1995 with the use of modified pickup trucks in the SuperTruck series. A year later, the series gained a major sponsor and has been known since as the NASCAR Craftsman Truck Series.

The Craftsman Truck Series is one of three national racing series sponsored by NASCAR. The others are the Sprint Cup (formerly Nextel Cup) and the Nationwide Series (formerly Busch Series).

HE SAID IT

"The Craftsman Truck Series is a good place to teach people to race hard. It is an awesome training ground and it is great to learn the big tracks."

— Kevin Harvick

have enough experience and his team didn't have the same resources as some of the others."[5]

Still, Harvick performed well enough that Spears made the commitment to backing him full-time on two circuits in 1998 – the national truck series and the NASCAR Winston West Series, a step up from the Featherlite Southwest Series. "He really wanted to drive cars," Hoffman said of the decision to give Harvick a chance in the Winston West Series.[6] A demanding schedule of hurrying from site to site to keep active in both series awaited Harvick and the Spears team.

NASCAR driver Kevin Harvick relaxes by playing with a radio-controlled gas-engine-powered truck.

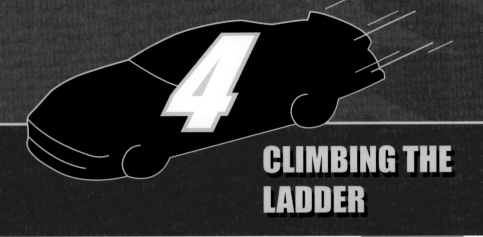

4
CLIMBING THE LADDER

Jerry Glanville left behind a career as a National Football League (NFL) coach to pursue success on the race track. Similar to Kevin Harvick, Glanville raced traditional stock cars and in the NASCAR Craftsman Truck Series.

Glanville was among the drivers in the field on February 25, 1998, when Harvick, then twenty-two years old, dominated the field at the Las Vegas Motor Speedway.

In his second NASCAR Winston West Series race of the

season—and just the sixth of his career—Harvick was untouchable. Harvick won the right to start on the pole by averaging 163.820 miles (263.64 kilometers) per hour in qualifying for the 150-mile (241.4-kilometer) Cactus Clash. He led the first forty-five and the last forty-four laps of the 100-lap race. The only time he was not in the lead was after a pit stop midway through the race.

"I never got close to him," said Glanville, the former coach of the NFL's Houston Oilers and Atlanta Falcons. "I had a shot at him, but he was smart. On the back straightaway, he was ruining the draft. And he threw it all off."[1] Glanville eventually settled for third behind Tony Toste. Harvick set a race record by averaging 110.565 miles (177.94 kilometers) per hour.

Las Vegas has a special place in Harvick's life. "Vegas is always going to be special to me because it's where DeLana and I got married," Harvick said. "We get to celebrate our anniversary out there every year.

QUALIFYING PROCESS

The starting order for most auto races is determined during timed qualifying trials. Cars race around the track individually and are timed, then placed in order, according to the best time.

I also have fond memories of the racetrack. That's where I won my first Winston West race. We always seem to run well out there."[2]

DID YOU KNOW?

The Houston Oilers, who started in the old American Football League, were a National Football League team before moving to Tennessee in 1997. The team, which played one season in Memphis before settling in Nashville, was known as the Tennessee Oilers before changing the nickname to Titans in 1999.

KEEPING BUSY

Harvick got what he was looking for when he increased his commitment to the sport a year earlier—a hectic racing schedule in 1998. Harvick went back-and-forth across the nation when necessary to run twenty-six races in the NASCAR Craftsman Truck Series, fourteen races in the NASCAR Winston West Series, and a dozen more on lower levels.

While struggling at times to keep up in the truck races, where he ranked seventeenth in the points standings on the national tour, Harvick was a force racing cars in the Winston West. The win in Las Vegas was the first of five in the season. He finished in the top five on six occasions and failed to do so just three times. In the last eight races of the season, he finished out of the top five just once.

Harvick and his wife DeLana listen to the national anthem prior to a race.

Auto racing is an expensive sport, but Harvick's effort in the two series brought in more than a half-million dollars in prize money. That showed he was on his way to making a career on the racetrack. Although he proved to be its best driver, Harvick said the Winston West Series had the competition necessary to prepare him to keep moving up.

"It is a series that is almost hidden," Harvick said. "It doesn't get a lot of media attention and there are a lot of race car drivers out there that are starting

KEVIN HARVICK'S NASCAR WINSTON WEST SERIES RESULTS

Year	Races	Wins	Top 5	Earnings
1996	1	0	0	$5,200
1997	3	0	0	$8,650
1998	14	5	11	$272,067
1999	1	0	1	$5,115
Total	19	5	12	$291,032

to get recognized. There are definitely a lot of good drivers hidden out there."[3]

With his performance, Harvick earned the series point championship and was named Motorsports Press Association Closed-Wheeled Driver of the Year. A different, more patient Harvick was developing behind the wheel. "Kevin learned patience," said Al Hoffman of Spears Racing, which sponsored Harvick in both series, "and, he learned to take it easy on the equipment. He ran the entire Winston West Series on one car."[4]

ON THE BRINK

The 1998 season showed Harvick was on the verge of breaking into the highest levels of race car driving. In the meantime, in 1999, he went out and had the best

A SPECIAL SEASON

A closer look at Kevin Harvick's five wins in the NASCAR Winston West Series in 1998:

CACTUS CLASH
Where: Las Vegas Motor Speedway
When: February 25
Length: 100 laps, 150 miles (241.4 kilometers)
Notes: The win was the first of Harvick's career on this level. He qualified for the pole for the first of five times in the season. The race finished under a caution flag.

SPEARS MANUFACTURING 200
Where: Altamont Motorsports Park
When: June 14
Length: 200 laps, 100 miles (160.93 kilometers)
Notes: Harvick never led until the last lap. He won by one second.

CALIFORNIA 200
Where: California Speedway
When: July 18
Length: 100 laps, 200 miles (321.87 kilometers)
Notes: Harvick won for the second time in three races. He started the race on the pole. He led laps 1–18, 62–76, and 82–100. He averaged more than 126 miles (202.78 kilometers) per hour.

KIDDE SAFETY 200
Where: Pikes Peak International Raceway
When: July 26
Length: 200 laps, 200 miles (321.87 kilometers)
Notes: Harvick won his second straight race in dominating fashion. He finished almost seven seconds ahead of the rest of the pack after leading the final ninety-two laps and 168 total.

IOMEGA/FRY'S 100
Where: Infineon Raceway
When: October 11
Length: 51 laps, 99 miles (159.33 kilometers)
Notes: Harvick's fourth win in six races. He led only the final lap and won the race by 0.154 seconds.

truck racing season of his career. Driving the Porter-Cable Power Tools Ford for new owner Jim Herrick, Harvick showed improvement in every statistical category. He finished in the top five six times and in the top ten a total of eleven times, at least doubling both numbers from the previous season. While running in all twenty-five races, Harvick led 214 laps. He reached a new high by finishing second at Mesa Marin, then matched that performance at Memphis and Nashville. When the season was over, Harvick had climbed to twelfth in the truck series final points standings.

With his new commitment to Herrick, Harvick ran just one Winston West race in 1999. He did, however, move up to the Busch Series for the first time, making one appearance, and he drove in two Automobile Racing Club of America (ARCA) races.

NEW TERRITORY

The Busch Series, which became the Nationwide Series in 2008, is NASCAR's second-highest, ranking just below the Cup series. It often pulls in many of those Cup series drivers as it serves as the warm-up to NASCAR's main event at the same site on the same weekend.

Harvick made his Busch debut October 23, 1999, in the Kmart 200 in Rockingham, North Carolina. He qualified twenty-fourth but had to settle

Harvick pits during the Dickies 500 race at Texas Motor Speedway in 2007.

for forty-second place, finishing next-to-last when he ran into engine problems after thirty-seven laps of a race that Mark Martin went on to win.

In his two ARCA appearances, Harvick finished second at Charlotte and third at Talladega.

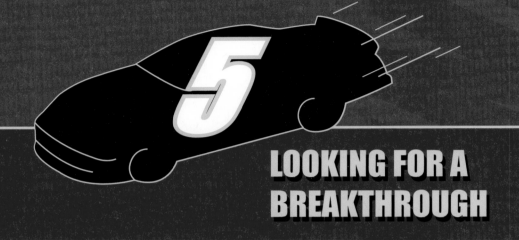

LOOKING FOR A
BREAKTHROUGH

Kevin Harvick's rookie season was more than halfway over when he moved into the lead late in the Carquest Auto Parts 250. Successful by just about any rookie driver standards, Harvick was becoming anxious for his first NASCAR Busch Series victory. Although he was racing at an average of more than 116 miles (186.68 kilometers) per hour, Harvick could not seem to get to the finish line at Gateway International Raceway fast enough.

Harvick celebrates a Busch Series win.

"The last 25 laps, every time I went by, I looked up at the scoreboard to make sure (the laps remaining) didn't go up instead of down," Harvick said. "There's been a lot of pressure we've put on ourselves the last three weeks. Nobody else put pressure on us. To finally get it over with, it's a weight off my back. We've been so close quite a few times, so I'm just happy to be here."[1]

PARKING THE TRUCK

Driving in the NASCAR Craftsman Truck Series has served its purpose for Harvick. It gave him the opportunity to show he was a quality racer, worthy of even better opportunities. Richard Childress, the owner of Dale Earnhardt's Cup car since 1984, noticed.

"We were at Martinsville (in 1999) when Richard Childress asked me about racing for him," Harvick said. "I was in the Porter Cable truck and still wasn't doing really well. The trucks were a great opportunity, but I never was on a team that had the same resources as the big ones had."[2]

Harvick parked the truck in 2000, sitting out the entire truck series to concentrate on racing cars. Although he would drop back in occasionally, making appearances in six of the next seven seasons, Harvick raced only twenty-three more times in the truck series during that period. By succeeding in his move to the

Busch Series, Harvick positioned himself to be primarily a race car driver for the remainder of his career.

Driving the AC Delco Chevrolet for Richard Childress Racing was a chance for Harvick to show just how good he could be. He had a second-place finish and two third-place finishes during a seven-race stretch in which he made the top eight six times. The frustration of failing to win may have shown the next three races, when Harvick failed to crack the top ten.

That all changed in Illinois with his first win. From then on, he was tough to stop.

BIG FINISH

The first win gave Harvick a strong start in the final dozen races of the 2000 season. He stayed among the contenders

FAVORITE TRACKS

Kevin Harvick's second career NASCAR Busch Series win came at Bristol Motor Speedway in Tennessee.

Bristol turned out to be one of Harvick's favorite tracks. By the end of the 2007 season, Harvick had five career wins on the three major NASCAR circuits on each of three different tracks—Bristol, Richmond International Raceway in Virginia, and Phoenix International Raceway in Arizona.

Harvick won four Busch races and a Cup race at both Bristol and Richmond. He won two truck races, two Cup races, and a Busch race at Phoenix.

for the next three races and made it back to the winner's circle in Bristol at the Food City 250, where he led 241 of 250 laps on the tight .533-mile (.86-kilometer) track.

Harvick controlled the entire race at Bristol, but had to be worried at the end when a restart turned the final two laps into a shootout. "All night long, I could ride as hard as I wanted to," Harvick said. "We had an awesome race car. It was flawless. I had no problem at all and that made for a pretty fun race."[3]

An accident with five laps remaining led to a red flag. All racing was stopped for seven minutes while the track was cleared. On a restart, the drivers remain in the order they were in prior to the red flag, but are bunched together like at the start of the race, making a change in position much more likely.

Jason Keller was in second place at the time of the restart, but his car stalled. NASCAR gave Keller time to get the car running, and set up the possibility of a close finish. Harvick ended the excitement when he jumped back out in front on the restart and held on for the last two laps to win by two car lengths. "When they said red flag, I was a little worried because Jason's car was pretty good there at the end," Harvick said. "I thought if he got a good jump he could get me, but once I got going it was all good."[4]

Harvick talks with car owner Richard Childress during practice for the Daytona 500 in 2008.

Harvick had one more win left in him before the 2000 season was over, on October 29 in the Sam's Town 250 in Memphis.

After qualifying second in Memphis, Harvick made winning difficult by jumping the start. He drew a penalty, forcing him into a stop-and-go pit stop that put him a full lap behind right from the beginning. He disagreed with the penalty—Harvick thought pole-sitter Jeff Green sat back rather than him starting too soon—but he tried to keep his cool and patiently work his way through the field. "When you get mad, get angry, and you start trying to overrun the car, mine usually ends up with the right front tire wrapped around the window," Harvick said. "So, it doesn't do a whole lot of good to get mad. You just put it behind you and keep going."[5]

Harvick took the lead on the 180th lap of the 250-lap race and held it as five cautions, including four in the final fifty laps, continually bunched the field. "We're fortunate that everything worked out for us today," Kevin said. "We got away with a mistake today, and we need to keep it from happening again."[6]

DID YOU KNOW?

When Kevin Harvick won three NASCAR Busch Series races in the 2000 season, he became just the second rookie to do so. Steve Park, in 1997, was the first to win that many.

ROOKIE OF THE YEAR

Mistakes are a given in a rookie season. Harvick and Richard Childress had an understanding on how to deal with them. "Not knowing what to expect, it's been a year of learning, from the time we started until now," Harvick said. "One thing Richard told me when we started was 'Don't make the same mistake twice. Every time you make a mistake, sit down and think about it, and don't do it again.'"[7]

Harvick used the lessons he learned to beat out his friend, Ron Hornaday Jr., for Rookie of the Year honors by finishing third in the final Busch Series points standings. Hornaday won a pair of races and finished fifth in

2000 NASCAR BUSCH SERIES POINTS STANDINGS

1.	Jeff Green	5,005
2.	Jason Keller	4,389
3.	Kevin Harvick	4,113
4.	Todd Bodine	4,075
5.	Ron Hornaday Jr.	3,870
6.	Elton Sawyer	3,776
7.	Randy LaJoie	3,670
8.	Casey Atwood	3,404
9.	David Green	3,316
10.	Jimmie Johnson	3,264

the overall points standings, two spots behind Harvick. The third-place finish by Harvick was tied for the best ever by a rookie, while the overall points total (4,113) and money earned ($995,274) represented rookie records.

FINDING SUCCESS

Kevin Harvick was a busy man in 2001. In the same year that he married DeLana, the crash that claimed the life of Dale Earnhardt doubled Harvick's racing schedule.

Harvick did more than just get through the sixty-nine-race schedule—he thrived on it. He won the NASCAR Busch Series championship and earned Rookie of the Year honors in the NASCAR Winston Cup Series.

Richard Childress put the future of his company in Harvick's hands. He told the twenty-five year

Harvick walks to the press conference to announce that he is taking over for the late Dale Earnhardt, Sr.

old that the team needed to do everything possible to make sure the 300-plus employees of Richard Childress Racing (RCR) did not have their lives disrupted as a result of Earnhardt's death. "For him and the race team to come back and perform the way they did was an unbelievable year," Childress said. "It just shows the strength of the race team and shows what Kevin Harvick is made of. There's not many people that can be put into that kind of situation and be able to come back and run that amount of miles and races and win the Busch Championship and then come back and accomplish the things he has in Winston Cup this year."[1]

Harvick did not have the option of failing—or the time to think about the implications of what happened if he did. In a way, he said, the hectic schedule and short notice may have helped remove some of the pressures a NASCAR Cup rookie would typically face.

"I don't have to prepare for anything like a normal rookie, because I . . . never had

DID YOU KNOW?

When Kevin Harvick first arrived in NASCAR's top racing series, it was known as the Winston Cup. The series began as Strictly Stock in 1949 and was known as NASCAR Grand National from 1950 to 1970. A sponsorship agreement changed the name to the Winston Cup from 1971 to 2003. The series was known as the Nextel Cup from 2004 to 2007. In 2008, the series name changed again, this time to the Sprint Cup.

to think about it," Harvick said. "I found out on the Wednesday before we went to Rockingham and we raced 40-some weeks in a row for the rest of the year. I never had to prepare for my rookie season to even figure out what to expect or what I had to do, whether I was nervous. I didn't know how much money I was making. I didn't know how many races I had to go to, I didn't have a contract. I didn't care."[2]

The season was more than halfway over before Harvick and Richard Childress got around to formalizing a Winston Cup contract. "Kevin Harvick helped RCR stay in business," Childress said.[3]

TOUGH COMPETITOR

It takes a special competitor to excel in the circumstances Harvick faced during the 2001 season. His competitiveness and the accomplishments that went with it earned wide-ranging praise. The racing style that produced those results, however, has had a tendency to get Harvick into his share of controversies. At various points in his career, Harvick has feuded with rival drivers.

"Richard Childress has probably had the most impact," Harvick said, when discussing adjustments to his racing strategy. "He's taught me how to drive for points. I used to drive for laps. Sometimes I forget or

Harvick holds up his trophy after winning a race in his rookie season of 2001.

get excited and I still do. But that doesn't get you a lot of wins. My dad used to tell me that, but I never paid attention to him."[4]

Although Harvick constantly worked on taking fewer chances to make sure he could finish more races, not everyone agreed that he became careful enough. "You race each other and you use a little class about it, or you can kind of be like a bull in a china closet and just run over people. He chooses to do the second," Ricky Rudd said after a particularly tough battle for the lead late in the 2001 Cup season.[5]

Jeff Green battled Harvick at the top of the Busch standings in 2000 and 2001. They were Cup teammates on Sundays in the second year of that battle, but it did not do much to change their relationship. "Anybody can turn somebody sideways to pass them," Green said. "He's done it way too much. Yeah, he's my teammate, but I don't like it."[6]

The frequency may have reduced, but there were more incidents later in Harvick's career. NASCAR banned Harvick from a Cup race in 2002 for punishment of his rough driving tactics in a Craftsman Truck Series race.

He endured multiple fines from NASCAR for rough driving, had another run-in with Rudd, and had disputes with Bobby Hamilton and Joe Nemechek. Harvick even wound up at odds with the RCR racing team, at times. He had to be coaxed back out of his trailer at Bristol in 2005 to reenter the race after the crew had finished repairs following a crash.

In a 2006 interview, he acknowledged that he could have handled some internal team issues in better ways. "I shouldn't have said things about the team," Harvick said. "I should have gone to Richard and said, 'this is how I feel' or gone to (crew chief) Todd Berrier and said, 'this is how I feel.' And they should be able to come to me.

"From that point, Bristol was one of the biggest lessons I've ever learned. I can't be a thorn in the side, causing commotion."[7]

Driving success and his commitment to the sport have generally helped Harvick overcome the controversies that have surfaced in his career. He said those that believe his aggressive driving style is an attempt to copy Earnhardt are mistaken. "If you look back to how I raced from the time I started, you would understand that's just how I am," he said.[8]

AN ENDURANCE TEST

The Nationwide Series and Sprint Cup Series are often, but not always, run at the same site. When they are not, running full-time in both series requires exhausting travel with quick plane rides between races at different sites on the same weekend.

Childress was confident in Harvick's ability to deal with the scheduling concerns. "He is a tough young guy. He is one of those guys who can handle pressure," the team owner said. "Pressure doesn't bother him, and if there is anyone out there who can do it, he can do it. He has his head on right. He is a good, smart young man."[9] Harvick never seemed to slow down in a season that featured 16,980 laps and 21,320 miles (34,311.21 kilometers) of racing.

In 2000, Harvick kept his planned commitment to the Busch Series while adding the Cup schedule as the emergency replacement in Earnhardt's Goodwrench-sponsored car. When he was done, Harvick had driven in sixty-nine high-level races in 2001. He made the final thirty-five races of the thirty-six-race Cup schedule, all thirty-three Busch races and even made one start in a Craftsman Truck race in Richmond. In that one truck appearance, Harvick finished second, adding to his year-long string of impressive accomplishments.

"We went into the year trying to run for the Busch Series Championship and obviously everything happened at Daytona and kind of turned our world upside down," Harvick said. "Everybody at RCR kind of regrouped and really put our heads together and just took the ball and ran with it. We did what we could and it's been a great year."[10]

Harvick was at the forefront and busy with both series, but members of each racing team and support from RCR were also important in helping him get through the season. "It's been quite an accomplishment, not only for myself but for everyone that's been involved in it, it's just been a phenomenal year and it says a lot for Richard Childress."[11]

SERIES CHAMPION

The day before Earnhardt's fatal crash, Harvick got his Busch Series season off to a positive start by finishing second to Randy LaJoie in the NAPA Auto

2001 BUSCH SERIES POINTS STANDINGS

1.	Kevin Harvick	4,813
2.	Jeff Green	4,689
3.	Jason Keller	4,642
4.	Greg Biffle	4,509
5.	Elton Sawyer	4,100
6.	Tony Raines	3,975
7.	Mike McLaughlin	3,962
8.	Jimmie Johnson	3,871
9.	Chad Little	3,846
10.	Kenny Wallace	3,799

FOUR MONTHS OF DOMINANCE

Kevin Harvick's performance in a span of fifteen races in the 2001 NASCAR Busch Series season:

Date	Race	Track	Start	Finish
4/28	Auto Club 300	Fontana	5	5
5/4	Hardee's 250	Richmond	12	5
5/12	CVS Pharmacy 200	Loudon	1	2
5/20	Nazareth 200	Nazareth	2	2
5/26	Carquest Auto Parts 300	Charlotte	1	26
6/2	MBNA Platinum 200	Dover	2	3
6/16	Outback Steakhouse 300	Kentucky	11	1
7/1	GNC Live Well 250	Milwaukee	1	4
7/8	GNC Live Well 200	Watkins Glen	6	3
7/14	Hill Brothers Coffee 300	Chicago	4	27
7/21	Carquest Auto Parts 250	Gateway	2	1
7/28	NAPA Autocare 250	Pikes Peak	8	3
8/4	Kroger 200	Indianapolis Raceway Park	12	1
8/18	NAPAonline.com 250	Michigan	7	2
8/24	Food City 250	Bristol	2	1

Parts 300 at Daytona. That was just the beginning. Harvick was second again at Rockingham in what could be regarded as a warm-up for his Winston Cup debut. By the time he was done, Harvick won five races and finished in the top five a remarkable twenty times in thirty-three races to win the points championship over Green, the 2000 champion.

Harvick sandwiched pole positions at Bristol and Nashville around his first win of the season at Fort Worth. After a rough outing at Talladega, he started a stretch in which he finished in the top five in eight out of the next nine and thirteen of the next fifteen races.

Just about the time Harvick could have figured to be battling exhaustion, he was at his best of the season. "We really didn't know what to expect," Harvick said. "We didn't know if we'd make it through July with all the flying back and forth or what the deal may be. We just kept going week-to-week and everything went really well."[12] The hot stretch culminated in three wins in five races, from July 21 to August 24, 2001.

Harvick started second in the Carquest Auto Parts 250 at Gateway International Raceway in Madison, Illinois, and got the win July 21. He followed Jeff Purvis and Jeff Green to the finish line in third place in the NAPA Autocare 250 at Pikes Peak International Raceway in Fountain, Colorado. Harvick was back on top in the Kroger 200, coming from the twelfth starting position to beat out Greg Biffle at Indianapolis Raceway Park in Clermont, Indiana. After finishing second to Ryan Newman at the NAPAonline.com 250

KEVIN AND DELANA GET MARRIED

In the aftermath of Dale Earnhardt's death, Kevin Harvick was unsure what to do next. He and DeLana Linville planned to get married later that month when the NASCAR circuit passed through Las Vegas.

With support from those around them, including team owner Richard Childress, Kevin and DeLana went ahead with their plans. Harvick explained the decision process in a diary that he wrote for sportsline.com.

"We'd been planning a Vegas wedding for months. But in light of everything that had just happened, we thought about postponing the wedding. We honestly didn't know what to do. After talking to a lot of friends and family, we decided to go ahead with it. I think Richard put it best. He said we all needed something happy to look forward to."

DeLana was familiar with life in auto racing. Her father, John Paul Linville, was a NASCAR Busch Series driver. She met Kevin while doing public relations work for Busch Series driver Randy LaJoie.

DeLana's understanding played a big part in helping Kevin get through a trying year. "Without her, I'm not sure I would have been able to handle all of this," he wrote.

at Michigan International Raceway, Harvick returned to the winner's circle. The streak concluded with a win by more than three seconds at Bristol, where he was more than two laps behind at one point in the Food City 250 before plowing through the field in a way that angered Green.

Harvick and his wife DeLana celebrate his victory in a 2007 Busch Series race.

"We had a flat tire and lost two laps," Harvick said. "We just put our heads down and were gonna take what we got. We made up the two laps, and we got through the field pretty good and were running 10th. Then a couple of them crashed, and we didn't have to pass three or four of them.

"The car was just awesome. Had to get a little bit aggressive with a couple of them, but it's Bristol. You've gotta do what you've gotta do."[13]

DID YOU KNOW?

Kevin Harvick moved back into the NASCAR Busch Series points lead after the fifteenth race of the 2001 season and stayed there the rest of the way, holding the lead through eighteen more events.

ROOKIE OF THE YEAR

On short notice, Harvick entered his first NASCAR Cup race and finished fourteenth at Rockingham. A week later, just days after he married DeLana, Kevin improved on that effort by placing eighth at Las Vegas.

Harvick won the Cracker Barrel Old Country Store 500 in Atlanta and was suddenly eleventh in the points standings after running three races to all the other contenders' four.

There was little doubt that Harvick was ready to compete. He finished second in the Coca-Cola 600 on Memorial Day weekend. About the same time he pulled away from the field in the Busch Series, Harvick also caught up to the leaders in the Winston Cup Series for good.

Just six days before taking off on his three-wins-in-five-races tear in the Busch Series, Harvick produced his second Winston Cup win. He beat the field in the Tropicana 400 when the Winston Cup made its debut at the new Chicagoland Speedway in Joliet, Illinois.

Harvick appeared to have one of the strongest cars throughout the race. He led for more than 100 of the 267 laps on the 1.5-mile (2.41-kilometer) track. Even though he was back in sixth place for a restart on lap 234, he was able to climb into the lead in just five laps. He got past Jimmy Spencer—then four other drivers—on his way to first place. "That was probably the toughest part," Harvick said. "I thought Spencer was the car to beat. And I knew he was going to be hard to pass. I saw an opportunity to make it three-wide and drive in on the bottom to get past, but with everyone else I was able to take some time and drive by them."[14]

By winning twice in the same season, Harvick eliminated any thoughts that his first win might have been a fluke. "This means a lot," he said. "When you get your first win, everybody says you're a flash in the pan. So here's a second win."[15]

The day after he was done ripping through the Busch Series, Harvick went back out at Bristol and took second in a Winston Cup race. He had another runner-up finish two races later in Richmond. It all added up to a ninth-place finish in the Winston Cup standings and another Rookie of the Year award. He was the only driver among the top ten in the final standings who did not appear in every race.

TIME TO REST

Even with all the success, Harvick was happy the season came to an end and he got a chance to rest. "I'm glad it's over—it's been a year of ups and downs," he said. "We sustained the highest of highs and the lowest of lows. We've got that yellow stripe on the back of the Winston Cup car, so that means we're on a pretty steep learning curve and we drew a lot of media attention. We ran the season under a microscope and I think it is going to make us a better team in the long run and I know it's made me a better driver in the one year we've dealt with it all."[16]

DID YOU KNOW?

When the NASCAR Busch Series postseason awards were given out in 2001, Richard Childress Racing's Lanny Barnes was named Clevite Engine Builder of the Year. Barnes built the engines used in Kevin Harvick's cars.

It all started with some hard lessons for a young man trying to make his mark in a thrilling, but dangerous, sport. "If there's one thing I've learned from this year — it's that life can change at any given time for anybody," Harvick said. "You take the icon of our sport and he's gone, just with the snap of a finger. I'm still the gung-ho guy and just go at it, but you kind of step back and you realize it can happen to anybody and no one is invincible."[17]

2001 WINSTON CUP SERIES POINTS STANDINGS

1.	Jeff Gordon	5,112
2.	Tony Stewart	4,763
3.	Sterling Marlin	4,741
4.	Ricky Rudd	4,706
5.	Dale Jarrett	4,612
6.	Bobby Labonte	4,561
7.	Rusty Wallace	4,481
8.	Dale Earnhardt Jr.	4,460
9.	Kevin Harvick	4,406
10.	Jeff Burton	4,394

Kevin Harvick made it through a grueling 2001 season and immediately worked out a plan with team owner Richard Childress. After becoming the first driver ever to win the Busch Series championship and Winston Cup Rookie of the Year honors in the same season, Harvick would cut back his schedule to concentrate on finding even more success on NASCAR's top level.

"Our goal next year is to win the championship," Harvick said. "That's the reason we cut our Busch schedule back to just a couple of races. We're going to go in full tilt and do everything we can to put ourselves in contention and just try and be there when it comes down to November next year and do everything we can to win a championship."[1]

The strategy seemed logical enough. The results over the next few years, however, did not necessarily go according to plan. The busier Harvick was, the more successful he was. He had his toughest season in 2002, when he almost cut the Busch Series out altogether.

Harvick competed in most, but not all, of the Busch races in four later seasons and was more successful. When he went back to full-time on both circuits in 2006, he had the best year of his career.

What seemed like a one-time venture, brought on by necessity, instead developed into a career path. Harvick did not see that coming as the 2001 season, which then seemed like an oddity in NASCAR, wrapped up. "It's been something that no one else has ever done and probably won't be done again," he said.[2]

TAKING A STEP BACK

Following a one-race suspension imposed by NASCAR early in the 2002 season, Harvick embarked on a streak of consecutive Cup race starts that had reached 244 at the end of 2008. Harvick's performance, particularly in terms of consistency, dropped off significantly from 2001. He ran thirty-five races each season. In 2001, he finished thirty-four races and was on the lead lap at the end of twenty-seven of them. In 2002, he finished twenty-nine races and was on the lead lap just thirteen times.

Harvick only had one fewer win and one fewer top-five finish than his rookie season. His top tens, however, were cut in half. As a result, Harvick plummeted from ninth to twenty-first in the 2002 final points standings.

An eight-race stretch in which he never finished higher than twenty-fifth left Harvick all the way down to thirty-fourth in the points standings as the midway point in the season approached. There was only one driver behind him who had raced as often; the rest were all those who bounced in and out of the Cup race schedule.

The recovery started with a fourteenth-place finish back home in California at Sonoma. Harvick salvaged the season during the next two weeks. He won the pole at Daytona for the July 6 Pepsi 400, where he led for thirteen laps and finished eleventh.

At Chicagoland in the following race, Harvick made it two-for-two in Cup events at the new track. He overcame a spin for his only Cup win of the season, repeating his title in the Tropicana 400. Harvick attempted to pass Kurt Busch on the apron on the

Harvick rests in the garage as his crew prepares the car.

inside of the track and went into a spin in lap 197 of the 267-lap race. Harvick managed to get his car under control while others crashed behind him, then he had time to get new tires during the resulting caution. "I just got down on the apron under Kurt," Harvick said. "He had somebody on the outside of him and, when I came up off the apron I just lost the air out of the back of the car and spun out."[3]

Harvick had become cynical after struggling much of the season and admitted that he was far from confident as he circled the track for the last time, looking to finish off the win. "I was just thinking, is the

Harvick (29) was in the middle of a wreck during the 2002 Daytona 500.

tire going to go flat, is the motor going to blow up, am I going to spin it out?" he said. "I spun it out once. What's going to go wrong now?"[4]

In many ways, the repeat Tropicana 400 title had Harvick looking like he had a year earlier. He was racing to success and irritating opponents along the way. Jeff Gordon, who wound up second, thought Harvick's spin was the result of an unnecessarily dangerous maneuver. "Pretty stupid move in my opinion," Gordon said. "He about took three-quarters of the field out when he did it."[5]

Harvick took a shot right back at Gordon from Victory Lane. "Jeff Gordon got second," he said. "Maybe if he had

THE IROC

The International Race of Champions (IROC) is auto racing's version of the All-Star game. Top drivers from each series are invited to perform in equal cars to see who is the best. Rules attempt to eliminate the advantage one crew can create and to make other team factors, such as pit stops, as insignificant as possible. The idea is to determine the best driver.

NASCAR drivers often do very well in IROC races. Kevin Harvick was invited to compete in the four-race series in 2002, 2003, and 2004. He won in Fontana, California, in the second race of the 2002 series, when the six NASCAR drivers finished in the top six spots, beating six other drivers, including Helio Castroneves and Al Unser Jr., in the field of twelve cars.

been a little braver, he would have won. He thinks it was a stupid move. I think it was pretty cool."[6] Childress was a bit more diplomatic, saying: "Race drivers today have to be bold. That's what it takes to win races, and I've seen Jeff Gordon make some of those moves and win races."[7]

The few times Harvick ventured elsewhere in 2002, he was more successful. He won once and was in the top five three times in four races in the prestigious International Race of Champions (IROC). He also raced in the Craftsman Truck Series five times and picked up his first career win there, along with a second- and a fourth-place finish.

DID YOU KNOW?

Both of Kevin Harvick's career wins in the NASCAR Craftsman Truck Series came at Phoenix in the Chevy Silverado 150. He posted his first win in 2002 then defended his title in 2003.

RETURNING TO BUSCH

After running just four Busch Series races in 2002, Harvick became more active in 2003, competing in nineteen of thirty-four races. His performance in both series improved dramatically.

The only thing that kept Harvick from threatening for the Busch points title was the fact that he did not go to the extremes of making every race. When he was in action, he was tough to stop. He earned the pole a career-high five times, won three races, finished in the top five a total of twelve times and was in the top ten all but once. After nine Busch starts, he had three wins, two seconds, and two thirds.

In the Cup Series, Harvick was having the best of his three seasons. He started a little slow and was eleventh in the points standings after fifteen of thirty-six races. He picked up the pace and finished fifth in 2003. Along the way, he became the first NASCAR driver to win the ten-year-old Brickyard 400 at famed

2003 BUSCH SERIES POINTS STANDINGS

1.	Matt Kenseth	5,022
2.	Jimmie Johnson	4,932
3.	Dale Earnhardt Jr.	4,815
4.	Jeff Gordon	4,785
5.	Kevin Harvick	4,770
6.	Ryan Newman	4,711
7.	Tony Stewart	4,549
8.	Bobby Labonte	4,377
9.	Bill Elliott	4,303
10.	Terry Labonte	4,162

Indianapolis Motor Speedway from the pole position. Harvick led the first seventeen and the last sixteen laps of the Brickyard 400, pulling away over the final ten laps to beat eventual season points champion Matt Kenseth by nearly three seconds. The win at Indianapolis started a streak of five straight races in the top five. Harvick closed out the year with his fifth runner-up finish of the season.

Harvick settled in to the middle of the Cup Series pack in the 2004 and 2005 seasons, finishing fourteenth in the standings both times. Whenever he raced in the Busch Series, he was one of the top threats to win, taking six more races during those two seasons.

BRISTOL SWEEP

As the first driver to run full-time in both the Busch Series and Cup Series in the same season, perhaps it was appropriate that Harvick should rule both on one of his favorite tracks. Harvick pulled off the "Bristol Sweep" in 2005, winning both races at the Bristol Motor Speedway in Tennessee on the same weekend.

The sweep came in a reverse order because the Busch race was postponed by rain and moved to Monday after Sunday's Cup race. Harvick rallied in each race. He ended a fifty-five-race winless streak with the Cup win. He then battled through a record fourteen

Harvick holds the trophy after a Busch Series race in 2003.

caution periods in the Busch race to edge Jeff Burton by .159 seconds. "It was one of those days where we bounced off the walls, had the fenders caved in and just kept going," Harvick said. "It was a pretty cool day."[8]

PLACE IN HISTORY

Harvick is regarded as one of the all-time great drivers in Busch Series history. When NASCAR polled fans and the media late in the 2006 season to determine the 25 Greatest Drivers in Busch Series history, Harvick was near the top of each list.

Fans placed Harvick third, behind only Mark Martin and Dale Earnhardt Jr. The media placed Harvick seventh. Martin led both lists. The poll was taken while Harvick was on his way to winning nine times in 2006, but before he added six more wins in 2007. With his recent pace, Harvick seems positioned to take a serious run at Martin's career record of forty-seven wins in the Busch Series. Harvick had thirty-two Nationwide Series wins through the 2008 season.

Mark Martin
Sam Ard
Dale Earnhardt Jr.
Jack Ingram
Dale Earnhardt
Harry Gant
Kevin Harvick
Tommy Houston
Randy LaJoie
Tommy Ellis
David Green
Greg Biffle
Jeff Green
Matt Kenseth
Bobby Labonte
Chuck Bown
Martin Truex Jr.
Jeff Burton
Larry Pearson
Jason Keller
Johnny Benson
Darrell Waltrip
Joe Nemechek
Rob Moroso
Dale Jarrett

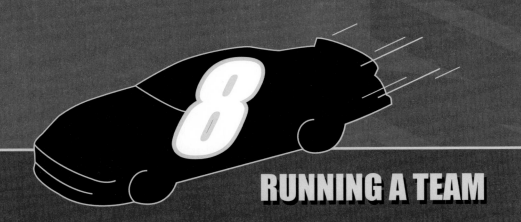

Kevin Harvick worked his way up in auto racing, literally at times. Early in his career, Harvick needed a place to stay while chasing his dream.

Ron Hornaday and his wife, Lindy, offered that place, allowing Harvick to spend months sleeping on a couch in the trophy room in their basement. When Hornaday was a driver looking for a team, Harvick was there for him.

Together, Harvick and Hornaday won the 2007 NASCAR Craftsman Truck Series championship with Harvick now in the lofty position of team owner and Hornaday behind the wheel. Harvick was actually in the race as well when Hornaday clinched the season points championship in the Ford 200 at Homestead, Florida. That put him in position to be the first one to Hornaday's car offering congratulations and sharing in the accomplishment.

"Ron Hornaday is the same type of person now as he was then," Harvick said, reflecting back to the time he was taken into the Hornaday home. "To share that moment with him on the backstretch and be the first person to congratulate him is something I'll never forget."[1]

There are times in auto racing when teamwork extends well beyond the mechanics and pit crew that prepare cars and beyond the financial support provided by sponsors and team owners. Harvick's special friendship with Hornaday made working together as a team even more meaningful. "For me, it's very personal," Harvick said. "I slept on Ron's couch a number of months trying to get a break in the sport. Lindy and Ron took me into their house, made me part of their family."[2]

Hornaday had won two previous Truck championships, but was a driver looking for work when Harvick brought him on board. The Truck series had seen seven different drivers win the previous seven titles. Hornaday made it eight winning drivers in eight

years when he won his third series title—and the first for Harvick's team.

Harvick showed loyalty, remembering Hornaday's early support, but also showed the skills of a successful team owner by recognizing a driver with the

Ron Hornaday's crew works on his truck during a 2007 race.

ability to win. "When Ron was out in the cold, looking for something to do, we had our truck team going and wanted to go forward," Harvick said. "I felt that Ron was the right person to put in there."[3]

2007 NASCAR CRAFTSMAN TRUCK SERIES POINTS LEADERS

1. Ron Hornaday   3,982

2. Mike Skinner   3,928

3. Johnny Benson   3,557

4. Todd Bodine   3,525

5. Rick Crawford   3,523

6. Travis Kvapil   3,511

7. Ted Musgrave   3,183

8. Matt Crafton   3,060

9. Jack Sprague   3,001

10. David Starr   2,921

TEAM BUILDING

Kevin and DeLana Harvick decided to invest in racing in a new way late in Harvick's successful 2001 season. They created Kevin Harvick, Inc. (KHI). Their first entry was in the Craftsman series with a truck built in a friend's garage. The team has seen major growth since then and has been housed in a 70,000-square foot facility in Kernersville, North Carolina, since 2004.

DeLana handles much of the day-to-day operation of the business and both are proud of its growth. "There's nothing that can quite describe the feeling that you have when it's your own team because we're there every day with these guys and see how hard they work," DeLana said.[4]

KHI moved into the Busch Series and increased the time it spent there. The team grew to the point that in 2007 it featured two Busch Series cars, driven by Bobby Labonte and Tony Stewart, and Hornaday's truck. "Owning a team is a lot like owning any other sports franchise," Harvick said. "It's taken us six years to get our truck team to where it's at."[5]

The team has expanded to about eighty employees, servicing the multiple teams and filling the new facility. "You're responsible for a lot of people," Harvick said. "And to see it start from one truck, a bunch of guys from RCR, and evolve into 70,000 square feet, four race teams, is something that's also very rewarding. To be a part of that as you've built it from basically dirt, from scratch, and see it evolve

THEY SAID IT

"They don't give these things away. We've been trying for an awful long time."
— Crew chief Rick Ren after Ron Hornaday's 2007 NASCAR Craftsman Truck series points title

into a championship-winning organization is very gratifying."[6]

Stewart drove two Busch races for KHI in 2004 and increased his commitment in 2005, getting the season off to a rousing start by winning the opening Hershey's Take 5 300 at Daytona. Harvick gives Stewart much of the credit for helping KHI grow. "He had a big part to do with where the evolution of the company and how it evolved into what it is today just because he wanted to drive those Busch cars and he wanted to drive them on our team," Harvick said.[7]

CHAMPIONSHIP RACE

Hornaday had won two previous titles, but those came back in 1996 and 1998. Just after the midway point in the 2007 season, Hornaday started picking up momentum. In a span of five races, he won twice and finished second two other times. That gave him four wins in the season.

Following a tough outing in Las Vegas where he finished twenty-second, Hornaday had two more second-place finishes and a third in the next five races to arrive at Homestead behind only Mike Skinner in the season points race.

After being behind Skinner by 164 points midway through the season, the gap was just twenty-nine entering the final race. "He's just a hard-core racer,"

Harvick said of Hornaday. "He grew up at Saugus Speedway racing on a one-third-mile [track]. He raced for everything that he's got. They made a living off of racing. They went in debt off of racing. They did everything that they did from racing. It's just always how he's been."[8]

Harvick (right) congratulates Hornaday after Hornaday won his third Truck Series championship in 2007.

HORNADAY-SKINNER RIVALRY

The Ron Hornaday-Mike Skinner rivalry has a long history on the NASCAR Craftsman Truck Series.

Hornaday qualified for the pole, but Skinner won the race in the very first truck race in Phoenix in 1995. They have combined for sixty-four victories in the series, with Hornaday winning thirty-nine. Skinner won twenty-five, including sixteen in the first two seasons when he won the first title, then finished third behind Hornaday for the next championship.

The two veterans traded the points lead six times in the final seven races of the 2007 season, with Hornaday emerging on top. "I don't think either one of us can walk away from here tonight and say, 'Ah, what a horrible year,'" Skinner said. "Because, it's been a great year."[9]

Hornaday, who had won just three series races between his second season title in 1998 and the start of the 2007 season, was back. However, he still needed help, in the form of struggles for Skinner, in order to pull out the championship in the final race. When Skinner had trouble with his right front tire early, then had the left rear wheel fall off later, an opportunity was there for Hornaday to overcome the twenty-nine-point deficit. Hornaday drove right through, taking seventh place. "I regret we didn't have a spare hub in the pits," said Skinner, who limped down pit road on three wheels, then returned to the race eleven laps later. "We took one off another housing, but it came down, it wasn't going to make any difference anyway."[10]

The season title was one that provided a special feeling for a lot of people. "Ron has done so much for Kevin, and to be able to give back to him, that's not a feeling that you can describe," DeLana said.[11]

THE TEAM'S FUTURE

By the time the championship evolved in 2007, Harvick was thrilled with the makeup of his dedicated KHI staff. "It's not easy to find people that care as much about your company as you do," he said. "But we've found those people and we're starting to put them in the right places. It's all about the people. It's not about having the fastest trucks. It is, but if you don't have the right people in the right place, it's never going to work."[12]

One of those "right people" is having DeLana in charge of so many of the business issues in order to allow Harvick to keep concentrating on his driving career. With twenty-one wins piling up in 2006 and 2007, Harvick still sees a lengthy driving career ahead.

That may keep KHI from moving too quickly into trying to put a team together for the Cup series. "The driving force is still the driving of the Nextel Cup car. I enjoy that," Harvick said after Hornaday clinched the 2007 truck series title. "I enjoy the Busch car. I enjoy the truck, but the competitor in me still likes to sit in the driver's seat and go out and race for wins and race for races on the racetrack. I'd have been a nervous wreck tonight sitting up on top of the pit box as an owner."[13]

With DeLana in charge, Harvick was able to be on the track that day. He drove in just six truck races in 2007, but finished in the top ten five times. He was fourth, finishing in front of Hornaday on the day the team he owned won the title.

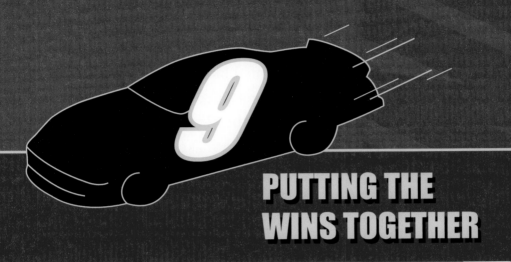

PUTTING THE WINS TOGETHER

Tony Stewart was well established as a road-course driver when he passed Kevin Harvick with six laps to go in the 2006 AMD at the Glen in Watkins Glen. Harvick had not proven yet that he could win on a road course.

Harvick, however, was not ready to back down. He kept right with Stewart until passing him on the inside with three laps to go to take his second Nextel Cup win of what was developing into a highly successful season.

"I don't know how he passed me," said Harvick, who had held the lead from laps fifty-eight through eighty-one of the ninety-lap race. "I knew my only shot to get him back was getting into (Turn) 1. He had to back off; it seemed like his car didn't have quite enough brakes getting in there."[1]

Stewart was one of the first to congratulate Harvick, reaching into the car to shake his hand. "He's a good friend of mine," Stewart said. "It's fun racing guys you can trust like that. He did an awesome job."[2]

Harvick (29) outlasted Tony Stewart (right) to win the Nextel Cup Series AMD at the Glen auto race in 2006.

Trying to catch a driver the caliber of Stewart added to the challenge. Stewart was the defending champion of the race and had posted a total of five earlier wins at Watkins Glen. "I knew I was only going to have a couple of chances, so I took my chance," Harvick said. "Off I went. It stuck and I went by. To race Tony, who's one of my good friends and somebody who's so good out on road courses, makes it that much more gratifying."[3]

DID YOU KNOW?

Kevin Harvick's first win at Watkins Glen came on a day when there were ten caution flags during the race, the most ever in the event.

There were multiple reasons for the August 13, 2006, win to rank as a special one in Harvick's mind. "Personally, it was a major accomplishment in my career," Harvick said. "We'd been able to win on all the different types of race tracks as we've gone through the years, but the road course thing, we always had this little cloud over us. We had been in contention to win and always had things happen. To finally do that was pretty satisfying."[4]

Proving he could do it against someone who is known as a bit of a road-course specialist just added to the meaning. "Any time you succeed at something, you don't want to have it handed to you," Harvick

KEVIN HARVICK'S NASCAR CUP SERIES WINS

Date	Race	Site
March 11, 2001	Cracker Barrel Old Country Store 500	Atlanta
July 15, 2001	Tropicana 400	Chicago
July 14, 2002	Tropicana 400	Chicago
August 3, 2002	Brickyard 400	Indianapolis
April 3, 2005	Food City 500	Bristol
April 22, 2006	Subway Fresh 500	Phoenix
August 13, 2006	AMD at the Glen	Watkins Glen
September 9, 2006	Chevy Rock and Roll 400	Richmond
September 17, 2006	Sylvania 300	Loudon
November 12, 2006	Checker Auto Parts 500	Phoenix
February 18, 2007	Daytona 500	Daytona

said. "It makes it a lot more rewarding to do it against somebody that had been winning all of the races there and been very successful on road courses. To go out and be able to race with Tony was lots of fun. In the end, it made it that much more rewarding."[5]

OUT IN FRONT

The win at Watkins Glen was one of many in 2006. Harvick matched his previous career total with five Cup wins, and earned nine more in the Busch Series, where he won his second points championship.

Harvick's season hit its peak a month later when he won back-to-back races and moved into the points lead in the Cup race for the first time in his career. The wins bridged the end of the regular season and the Chase for the Cup, NASCAR's version of the playoffs.

Harvick won the 2006 Chevy Rock and Roll 400 at Richmond on September 7 in the last race before the Chase began. Harvick needed a solid finish in the race to secure his spot in the Chase, and the win ended any doubt.

With the top ten in the standings bunched close together, Harvick was in position to go for the points lead in New Hampshire. All pre-race signs were positive as Harvick had the fastest car in both practice sessions and led the way in

2006 BUSCH SERIES POINTS STANDINGS

1.	Kevin Harvick	5,648
2.	Carl Edwards	4,824
3.	Clint Bowyer	4,683
4.	Denny Hamlin	4,667
5.	J. J. Yeley	4,487
6.	Paul Menard	4,075
7.	Kyle Busch	3,921
8.	Johnny Sauter	3,794
9.	Greg Biffle	3,789
10.	Reed Sorenson	3,670

HOW THE NASCAR POINTS SYSTEM WORKS

NASCAR uses a points system, based primarily on the place finish in each race, to determine its overall champion each season. That system was adjusted slightly prior to the start of the 2007 season to add more emphasis to actually winning races.

The adjustments were made as NASCAR continued to seek balance between rewarding winning and consistency. "Winning is what this sport is all about," CEO Brian Francis said in a story on nascar.com. "Nobody likes to see drivers content to finish in the top 10. We want our sport—especially during the Chase—to be more about winning."

The winner of each race is awarded 185 points, an increase from the 180 that were awarded prior to 2007. The runner-up gets 170 points and the points drop throughout. For example: fifth place earns 155; tenth place receives 134; twenty-first place receives 100; thirtieth place receives 73; on down to forty-third place, which receives 34 points.

A bonus of five points is issued to any driver who leads at the end of at least one lap during the race. The driver who leads the most laps in a race receives an additional five bonus points.

Points are accumulated throughout the entire season, but since 2004 there has been an adjustment after the twenty-sixth race to attempt to add a playoff-type atmosphere to the Chase for the Cup. During the first three years, NASCAR tightened the standings between the top ten drivers and any other drivers within 400 points of the standings lead. That switched to simply the top twelve drivers in 2007.

Drivers need to be in the top twelve with ten races left to be eligible to win the all-season championship in the Chase for the Cup. The drivers on that list have their point total adjusted, making for a closer race heading into the stretch run of the season. Beginning in 2007, an additional factor involving total wins to that point was added to the equation for adjusting point totals.

"These changes should make the chase for the championship even more exciting for the race fans and more competitive for the teams," said Richard Childress, the owner of Kevin Harvick's Cup race team.

Harvick admires his trophy after winning the 2006 Chevy Rock and Roll 400.

qualifying to grab the pole position for the first time all season.

Nothing changed when the Sylvania 300 got started at New Hampshire International Speedway. Harvick jumped right into the lead before Jeff Gordon, who started on the outside of the first two, took over the lead on Lap 28. Harvick moved back into the lead on Lap 30 and led five more times before the day was over. He led the final eighty-four laps and a total of 196 out of 300 in the race.

The drivers got the green flag with thirty laps remaining with Harvick in front, followed by Brian Vickers, Jeff Gordon, and Jeff Burton. All four leaders needed tires, and when they emerged from their series of pit stops, Harvick had a commanding 2.5-second lead. That lead was minimized with four laps to go when Kyle Petty blew an engine, leading to a yellow flag and one final restart. Jeff Gordon and Tony Stewart kept after Harvick, and Stewart passed Gordon

2006 NASCAR NEXTEL CUP POINTS STANDINGS

1.	Jimmie Johnson	6,475
2.	Matt Kenseth	6,419
3.	Denny Hamlin	6,407
4.	Kevin Harvick	6,397
5.	Dale Earnhardt Jr.	6,328
6.	Jeff Gordon	6,256
7.	Jeff Burton	6,228
8.	Kasey Kahne	6,183
9.	Mark Martin	6,168
10.	Kyle Busch	6,027

into second, but neither was able to move to the lead.

"Those guys are on a roll and on a high," Gordon said. "It's up to us and other guys (going) for the championship to try to break some of that momentum."[6]

Harvick left New Hampshire and headed for Dover with a thirty-five-point lead over Denny Hamlin and a forty-one-point lead on Matt Kenseth. Harvick added one more win late in the season and went on to the best finish of his career, taking fourth in the final points standings. The five Cup wins tied for second-most on the season with Stewart and Jimmie Johnson, behind only Kasey Kahne. Harvick's fifteen top-five finishes tied for the most with Kenseth and Stewart.

SWEEPS

Kevin Harvick swept both the Busch Series and Cup Series races in the same weekend twice in 2006, doubling up at Phoenix and Richmond. With the two early-season wins at Phoenix, he became the first driver to win races there in all three major NASCAR circuits, including the Craftsman Truck Series.

KEVIN HARVICK'S BUSCH/NATIONWIDE SERIES CAREER STATISTICS

Year	Races	Wins	Top 5	Poles	Earnings	Points Rank
1999	1	0	0	0	$6,730	134
2000	31	3	8	2	$652,805	3
2001	33	5	20	4	$919,167	1
2002	4	0	0	0	$66,900	64
2003	19	3	12	5	$584,170	16
2004	22	2	10	0	$602,725	20
2005	21	4	14	2	$884,293	18
2006	35	9	23	1	$1,345,380	1
2007	26	6	11	2	$1,123,130	4
2008	22	0	8	1	$586,195	18
Total	214	32	106	17	$6,731,495	NA

ANOTHER BUSCH TITLE

Harvick simply destroyed the competition in the Busch Series in 2006. He won the title by a record margin of 824 points, clinching the championship four races before the season ended. Harvick won nine Busch races and finished in the top five twenty-three times. He was in the top ten in thirty-two races total, including the last eighteen in a row. Only Sam Ard, with ten in 1983, has won more races in a Nationwide season.

The only lap that Harvick did not complete in the entire 2006 Busch season was on October 13, the day he clinched the season championship at Lowe's Motor Speedway in Charlotte. He finished ninth in the race, one lap behind the leaders. As he did in the Cup series, Harvick even won back-to-back races at one point. When it was over, he was one of seven drivers to win at least two Busch season titles, joining Ard, Dale Earnhardt Jr., Jack Ingram, Randy LaJoie, Larry Pearson, and Martin Truex Jr.

"We enjoyed every minute this year," Harvick said. "I think the second time around, we're a lot more aware of how hard things are to come by in this sport."[7]

DAYTONA 500 CHAMPION

Kevin Harvick pulled up alongside Mark Martin in Turn 3 at Daytona International Speedway. Behind Harvick and Martin, cars were not just next to, but were actually slamming into each other. The two leaders progressed toward the finish line of the 2007 Daytona 500, safe from the crash behind them, but not necessarily unaffected.

As Harvick and Martin came to the end of a 500-mile race just feet apart, major decisions were unfolding around them.

Harvick made it to the finish line two-hundredths (0.02) of a second before Martin in what was the closest Daytona 500 since NASCAR went to electronic timing in 1993. The race was not close just because of the distance and time separating the two lead cars. The decisions being made in the seconds

Harvick [left] and Martin race to the finish line at the Daytona 500.

before and after Harvick and Martin got to the finish line were also extremely close calls that could go either way.

NASCAR race officials had to decide whether to switch from a green flag to bring the drivers to the finish line under a yellow caution flag. The caution flag, however, did not come down until after Harvick and Martin passed by the checkered flag that signifies the end of the race for the winner.

Even after they passed by, race officials technically could have gone back and determined that racing had stopped with the crash. No such decision was made, giving Harvick the thrilling victory for the biggest win of his career. In the process, Martin, the veteran fan favorite, was deprived a chance to break through and win the Daytona 500 for the first time on his twenty-third start in NASCAR's most famous and prestigious race.

"I knew I was going to be the bad guy at the end with Mark leading," Kevin said. "But we kept the pedal down and hoped for the best."[1]

The thrilling finish capped a week filled with controversy at Daytona, the showcase event which opens each NASCAR season. "This had to be the wildest Daytona 500 I've ever watched," said Richard Childress, the owner of Harvick's racing team. "I kept my eyes shut for a while there."[2]

LOOKING FOR AN EDGE

Controversy surrounded Daytona in the two-week build-up to what is also known as "The Great American Race." Several teams were caught cheating, including two-time champion Michael Waltrip, whose team was caught tampering with fuel. NASCAR dealt with the cheating by suspending five crew chiefs, punishing the teams of Waltrip, Kasey Kahne, Matt Kenseth, Scott Riggs, and Elliott Sadler. "Anytime there's a good race on the racetrack, it helps mend things. But I think it's still going to take a little bit to get over some of the issues that happened," Harvick said.[3]

Harvick enjoyed some success as he prepared for the Daytona 500. He won the Orbitz 300 Busch Series race from the thirty-first starting position. He entered the main event in the thirty-fourth starting position. The lowest any Daytona 500 winner had ever started up to that point was Bobby Allison in thirty-third in 1978.

DID YOU KNOW?

The 2007 Daytona 500 may not have been the closest in race history. In 1959, before the electronic timing that told us Kevin Harvick beat Mark Martin by 0.02 seconds, Lee Petty and Johnny Beauchamp came to the finish line at practically the same time. NASCAR needed to view various photo angles for three days before officially declaring that Petty had won the race.

UNEVENTFUL START

Tony Stewart and Kurt Busch took turns controlling the early part of the race. Stewart even made it back to the lead after dropping to fortieth place when he was penalized for speeding out of pit road. Then, Stewart and Busch got tangled up and the entire race changed.

Stewart and Busch went into the wall together in Turn 4 with forty-eight laps left, representing the first in a series of four major accidents late in the Sunday night event. After combining to lead for 130 of the first 152 laps, they were both out of the race.

Each of the wrecks involved at least three drivers. In all, more than half the cars—twenty-two out of forty-three—received at least some damage in one of the four late accidents.

2007 DAYTONA 500 TOP 10 FINISHERS

1. **Kevin Harvick**

2. **Mark Martin**

3. **Jeff Burton**

4. **Mike Wallace**

5. **David Ragan**

6. **Elliott Sadler**

7. **Kasey Kahne**

8. **David Gilliland**

9. **Joe Nemechek**

10. **Jeff Gordon**

DAYTONA SWEEP

Kevin Harvick became the fourth driver to sweep the NASCAR Busch Series race and Daytona 500 in the same weekend, joining Bobby Allison (1988), Darrell Waltrip (1989), and Dale Earnhardt Jr. (2004).

LeeRoy Yarbrough had a different sweep, winning the late model race and Daytona 500 in 1969, prior to the start of Busch Series racing.

"The demons came out when it got dark," Harvick said. "The entire complexion of the race changed because everyone's car handled better. We were three-wide, beating and banging. It was survival of the fittest."[4]

GOING OVERTIME

Jimmie Johnson went out in a crash with twenty-seven laps to go, then Dale Earnhardt Jr. got caught up in a pile of cars with five laps left. As the cars were sorted out from the latest crash, NASCAR brought out a red flag to stop racing entirely, leading to a restart that technically extended the race to 505 miles with an extra two laps of the 2.5-mile (4.02-kilometer) track.

Harvick, in his Number 29 car, still had been sitting in twenty-ninth place with just twenty laps left. After Earnhardt Jr.'s wreck, the cars were parked for almost twelve minutes, then lined up for a two-lap spring to the finish. Harvick was sixth on the restart, but feeling like he had a strong car with a chance. When the green flag came back out, he shot the pack quickly in pursuit of Martin, who was first on the restart. "We had such a run back there that I was coming like a freight train," Harvick said. "We were up against the wall and it was take what we could take. There was no holding back at that point."[5]

FINAL LAP

What happens behind them is not usually a concern for a race car driver with the checkered flag of victory in sight. This time, however, it meant everything to the forty-eight-year-old Martin, who was no stranger to racing heartbreak. A four-time Cup series points runner-up who has never won the all-season title, Martin was in position to break Dale Earnhardt's record of the longest wait for a first Daytona 500 win. Earnhardt won in his twentieth try in 1998, three years before he died at the end of the same race.

Cars were breaking apart and sliding off the track and Clint Bowyer was upside down. Pole-sitter David Gilliland, Jeff Gordon, David Stremme, Casey

Mears, Sterling Marlin, and Matt Kenseth were also caught up in the final-lap crash. "I saw Clint on his roof and it was just nuts," Stremme said. "At the end, all of a sudden people were coming from everywhere, going places they shouldn't be going and driving like they shouldn't be driving. It was crazy, but it didn't surprise me a lot."[6]

Overlooking the finish line, NASCAR officials had a split-second decision to rival nearly any in sports. They had to decide the racing equivalent of a block/charge foul call with a basketball game on the line in overtime or a safe/out call at home plate in extra innings—and all with nearly 200,000 fans looking on and millions more watching on television.

DAYTONA 500 MULTIPLE WINNERS

Richard Petty was the King of the Daytona 500, winning it a record seven times. Only eight drivers ever won the race more than once. The list of most wins in Daytona 500 history:

Richard Petty	7
Cale Yarbrough	4
Bobby Allison	3
Jeff Gordon	3
Dale Jarrett	3
Bill Elliott	2
Sterling Marlin	2
Michael Waltrip	2

Typically, a yellow flag goes up immediately when there is danger on the track. NASCAR, however, prefers to have the winner decided during live racing. That was the reason for the two-lap sprint in the first place.

In a matter of seconds the race would be over anyway. At Talladega in 2005, Dale Jarrett won in Mark Martin's position as the leader at the time of the crash and Stewart lost out in Harvick's spot as the first to the finish line, but there was more time between the crash and the finish in that race.

The drivers kept racing toward the finish and the yellow flag did not go up until right after the two leaders came through, with Harvick on the outside, about four feet ahead. "They waited! They waited! I can't believe they waited!" Martin said over the radio used to communicate with his crew. "I really thought that thing was ours, guys. It still might be."[7]

Harvick had a different reaction in his car. Seconds after those behind him dealt with fire, missing hoods, and body damage, Harvick's car was in need of a very simple repair. "I got so excited at the end of the race, and I knew we had won," he said. "I just didn't realize how excited I was, and I punched the dang mirror out of the car. Just overexcited, I guess. Knocked the mirror right out."[8]

Clint Bowyer crosses the finish line upside down.

THE AFTERMATH

NASCAR added confusion to the final decision in the few minutes after the race. An initial announcement said yellow had come out before the finish line, but after Harvick had taken the lead. That statement was later retracted and Harvick was named winner for getting to the finish line first. NASCAR officials also explained that there was no need to immediately freeze racing because in the first few seconds of the accident, the cars involved went off the track and were not a danger to other racers.

True to his reputation, Martin handled the decision with class. "Nobody wants to hear a grown man cry," he said. "I'm not going to cry about it. That is what it is and that's it. That's the end. They made the decision, and that's what we're going to live with."[9]

Jeff Burton, a current teammate of Harvick's and a former teammate of Martin's, followed them to the finish line in third place. While happy for his new teammate, Burton acknowledged disappointment for Martin. "It would be nice to see the hardware on his trophy case," Burton said. "He has so much respect, not only as a competitor but a person. He's a world-class individual."[10]

Harvick understood the sentiment. "When I got out of the car, I knew I wasn't going to be the good guy," he said. "Mark is one of the best people you'll ever meet. He's one of the best drivers who ever sat in the seat."[11]

2007 SEASON RECAP

The Daytona 500 is just the beginning of the NASCAR season. After winning the race on the sixth anniversary of Earnhardt's death, Harvick still had a full Cup schedule and most of a Busch schedule ahead. He was unable to produce another Cup win, but did race well enough to qualify for the Chase for the Nextel Cup, winding up tenth overall. "We've had everything under the sun go wrong and we've still been able to be part of the Chase and be competitive with everything that hasn't gone right," Harvick said. "I look at 2002 and I compare it to this year, and they're very similar years but we're a more mature team to make the results better."[12]

Harvick's status as one of the best Busch Series drivers of all time remained intact. He won six of twenty-six Busch starts and finished fourth in the final points standings despite sitting out nine races.

The dozens of other wins, however, are nothing like the status change that goes with being a Daytona 500 champion. "I've been fortunate to win the Brickyard 400, but there's nothing that matches the Daytona 500," Harvick said. "It has an effect worldwide. There's a lot more to it than a lot of people realize. It's something I've kind of had to learn."[13]

The double duty in the Cup and Busch Series is just one development that Harvick would have had a hard time anticipating six years earlier. The growth of KHI and the team Truck Series championship as an owner are two more. Fate seemed to deal Harvick a cruel blow when it took away his mentor in the 2001 Daytona 500 crash, but the way he dealt with the aftermath of that tragedy helped define his career.

"It's kind of hard to look back and say you wouldn't have anything that you have now, but I don't

think it would have happened as fast as it has, to be at a point in my career and my life to be 30 years old, own the race teams and be in the Cup series going on six years and won a Busch championship, an owners championship, a rookie of the year," Harvick said. "I don't think everything would have happened near as fast as it has. It would have been a much longer road."[14]

ANOTHER CHASE

The only thing missing from Harvick's highly successful 2008 season was a victory. His fourth-place

2007 NASCAR NEXTEL CUP STANDINGS

1. Jimmie Johnson 6,723
2. Jeff Gordon 6,646
3. Clint Bowyer 6,377
4. Matt Kenseth 6,298
5. Kyle Busch 6,293
6. Tony Stewart 6,242
7. Kurt Busch 6,231
8. Jeff Burton 6,231
9. Carl Edwards 6,222
10. Kevin Harvick 6,199
11. Martin Truex Jr. 6,164
12. Denny Hamlin 6,143

Harvick holds the trophy after winning the Daytona 500 in 2007.

CRAFTSMAN SUCCESS IN PHOENIX

Harvick's success in the Craftsman Truck Series continued in 2008. He claimed his first victory in the Truck Series in five years when he won at Phoenix International Raceway in November.

In fact, all three of Harvick's Truck Series titles have been won in Phoenix. The 2008 victory was especially memorable, though, since Harvick won as a member of the team he owns, Kevin Harvick Inc.

The victory was the third in a row for his truck team. Ryan Newman had won two weeks earlier, and Ron Hornaday, Jr. was victorious the previous week. It was the first time in the Truck Series that three different drivers from the same team had won consecutive races.

finish in the points standings was an improvement over his tenth-place standing in 2007 and equaled the highest of his career.

However, the 2008 season was the first time since 2004 that Harvick had been unable to claim a race victory. Even so, he was always contending, and placed among the top ten in nineteen of the thirty-six races in which he competed.

Harvick began the 2008 season by finishing in the top ten in four of the first five races. Then he missed the top ten in all but one of the next thirteen races. His thirty-seventh place finish at the Brickyard in the twentieth race of the season pushed him back to thirteenth in the points standings—out of the running for the Chase for the Cup. He would need to gain some ground in order to qualify as one of the top twelve drivers for the Chase. With that in mind, he rattled off six straight top-ten finishes to get into eleventh place, good enough by one place to qualify for the Chase.

"We don't give up, I can promise you that," Harvick said after the success at Pocono. "We stick in there and fight, even when they tell us we're done."[15]

It was the beginning of another surge. He went on to post top-ten finishes in nine consecutive races. That helped him climb up to fifth place in the points race. A second-place finish in the season's final race left Harvick in fourth overall.

The win at the 2007 Daytona remained his most recent victory, but he had made his presence felt throughout the 2008 season.

CAREER STATISTICS

Year	Rank	Starts	Wins	Poles
2008	4	36	0	0
2007	10	36	1	0
2006	4	36	5	1
2005	14	36	1	2
2004	14	36	0	0
2003	5	36	1	1
2002	21	35	1	1
2001	9	35	2	0

Top 5	Top 10	Earnings	Points
7	19	$5,603,650	6,408
4	15	$7,494,590	6,199
15	20	$6,201,580	6,397
3	10	$4,970,050	4,072
5	14	$4,739,010	4,228
11	18	$4,994,250	4,770
5	8	$3,748,100	3,501
6	16	$3,716,630	4,406

CAREER ACHIEVEMENTS

- **Was champion of the Winston West Series in 1998.**

- **Was named Busch Series Rookie of the Year in 2000.**

- **Earned his first Busch Series championship in 2000.**

- **Was named Winston Cup Series Rookie of the Year in 2001.**

- **Won his second Busch Series championship in 2006.**

- **Earned a fourth-place finish in Nextel Cup points standings in 2006.**

- **Won the Daytona 500 in 2007.**

- **The Craftsman Truck Series truck he owns won the series championship in 2007.**

- **Earned his second fourth-place finish in the Sprint Cup in 2008.**

FOR MORE INFORMATION

WEB LINKS

Kevin Harvick's official Web site:
http://www.kevinharvick.com

Kevin Harvick's nascar.com Web page:
http://www.nascar.com/drivers/dps/kharvick00/cup

Kevin Harvick Inc.'s official Web site:
http://www.kevinharvickinc.com

FURTHER READING

Doeden, Matt. *Kevin Harvick*. Mankato, Minn.: Capstone Press, 2009.

Leslie-Pelecky, Diandra. *The Physics of NASCAR*. New York: Dutton, 2008.

Martin, Mark, and Beth Tuschak. *NASCAR for Dummies*. Hoboken, N.J.: Wiley, 2005.

Roza, Greg. *Kevin Harvick: NASCAR Driver*. New York: Rosen Publishing, 2009.

CHAPTER NOTES

CHAPTER 1. REPLACING A LEGEND

1. Don Coble, "Seat belt to blame in death NASCAR officials say," AugustaChronicle.com, February 24, 2001. <http://chronicle.augusta.com/stories/022401/oth_MNS-8491.000.shtml> (November 26, 2007).

2. "Dale Earnhardt, 1951-2001: Childress Racing Holds News Conference on Crash Aftermath," CNN Transcript, February 23, 2001. <http://transcripts.cnn.com/TRANSCRIPTS/0102/23/se.04.html> (September 24, 2007).

3. B. Duane Cross, "Earnhardt's death wasn't the cruelest news three years ago," cnnsi.com, n.d.. <http://robots.cnnsi.com/2004/writers/b_duane_cross/02/17/dale.earnhardt/index.html> (November 26, 2007).

4. Mike Fish, "End of an era. Earnhardt's death high price for fans' excitement," cnnsi.com, February 18, 2001. <http://sportsillustrated.cnn.com/motorsports/2001/daytona500/news/2001/02/18/nascar_earnhardt_dies/> (September 24, 2007).

5. "Dale Earnhardt, 1951-2001: Childress Racing Holds News Conference on Crash Aftermath," CNN Transcript, February 23, 2001. <http://transcripts.cnn.com/TRANSCRIPTS/0102/23/se.04.html> (September 24, 2007).

6. Ibid.

7. Ibid.

8. "Kevin Harvick's Atlanta Performance History," Shell Racing Web site, March 18, 2007. <http://www.shell.com/home/content/us-en/society_environment/sports/shell_nascar/stats/previews/preview_atlanta.html#0 (September 25, 2007).

9. Ken Willis, "No Excuses Necessary – Kevin Harvick, racing car driver," *Auto Racing Digest*, September, 2001. <http://findarticles.com/p/articles/mi_m0FCH/is_5_29/ai_75753329> (September 25, 2007).

CHAPTER 2. EARLY START

1. "Driven to win," Kevin Harvick Web site, n.d., <http://www.kevinharvick.com/biography1.htm> (November 26, 2007).

2. Jerry F. Boone, "The Sky's The Limit," Stockcarracing.com, n.d., <http://www.stockcarracing.com/thehistoryof/37558_kevin_harvick_biography/index.html> (November 23, 2007).

3. Ibid.

4. Ibid.

5. Marty Smith, "Harvick crowned king of Busch," Turner Sports Interactive on NASCAR.com, January 14, 2002. <http://premium.nascar.com/2002/NEWS/01/11/banquet_story/index.html> (November 28, 2007).

CHAPTER 3. DECISION TIME

1. Jerry F. Boone, "The Sky's The Limit," Stockcarracing.com, n.d., <http://www.stockcarracing.com/thehistoryof/37558_kevin_harvick_biograph y/index.html> (November 23, 2007).

2. "Driven to win," Kevin Harvick Web site, n.d., <http://www.kevinharvick.com/biography1.htm> (November 26, 2007).

3. Jerry F. Boone, "The Sky's The Limit," Stockcarracing.com, n.d., <http://www.stockcarracing.com/thehistoryof/37558_kevin_harvick_biograph y/index.html> (November 23, 2007).

4. Ibid.

5. Ibid.

6. Ibid.

CHAPTER 4. CLIMBING THE LADDER

1. Chris McManes, "Harvick sets record in first victory," Las Vegas Review Journal Web site, February 26, 1998. <http:// www.reviewjournal.com/lvrj_home/1998/Feb-26-Thu-1998/sports/ 7033501.html> (November 27, 2007).

2. "UAW-DaimlerChrysler 400 – Kevin Harvick Notes," Race2Win.net, February 25, 2003. <http://www.race2win.net/wc/03/race/lvms/kh.html> (November 27, 2007).

3. "Kevin Harvick Chat Transcript," nascar.com, February 16, 2001. http://premium.nascar.com/2001/FANS/fannews/02/16/harvick_transcript /index.html (November 27, 2007).

4. Jerry F. Boone, "The Sky's The Limit," StockCarRacing.com. n.d., <http://www.stockcarracing.com/thehistoryof/37558_kevin_harvick_biograph y/index.html> (November 23, 2007).

CHAPTER 5. LOOKING FOR A BREAKTHROUGH

1. Associated Press, "Harvick continues Busch trend of rookie winners," ESPN.com, July 30, 2000. <http://espn.go.com/auto/nascar/ news/2000/0729/658675.html> (November 27, 2007).

2. Jerry F. Boone, "The Sky's The Limit," StockCarRacing.com, n.d., <http://www.stockcarracing.com/thehistoryof/37558_kevin_harvick_biograph y/index.html> (November 23, 2007).

3. Associated Press, "Rookie Harvick wins second race," ESPN.com, August 25, 2000. <http://espn.go.com/auto/nascar/news/2000/ 0825/704251.html> (November 27, 2007).

4. Ibid.
5. Bill Kiser, "Fast Learner," SceneDaily.com, November 2, 2000. <http://www.scenedaily.com/stories/2000/10/30/busch_coverage1.html> (November 28, 2007).
6. Ibid.
7. Ibid.

CHAPTER 6. FINDING SUCCESS

1. Pete McCole, "Harvick's amazing 2001 season," AutoRacing1.com, November 27, 2001. <http://www.autoracing1.com/NASCAR/PeteM/2001/1127HarvickSeason.htm> (November 29, 2007).
2. Brant James, "How a rookie helped a team cope," *St. Petersburg Times* Web site, February 18, 2006. www.sptimes.com/2006/02/18/Sports/how_a_rookie_helped_a.shtml (November 28, 2007).
3. Ibid.
4. Jerry F. Boone, "The Sky's The Limit," StockCarRacing.com, n.d., <http://www.stockcarracing.com/thehistoryof/37558_kevin_harvick_biography/index.html> (November 23, 2007).
5. Pete McCole, "Harvick's amazing 2001 season," AutoRacing1.com, November 27, 2001. <http://www.autoracing1.com/NASCAR/PeteM/2001/1127HarvickSeason.htm> (November 29, 2007).
6. Rick Houston, "'That's Bristol,'" scenedaily.com, September 3, 2001. http://www.scenedaily.com/stories/2001/09/03/busch_coverage2.html (November 29, 2007).
7. Al Pearce, "All Grown Up: Witness the new, more mature, Kevin Harvick," AutoWeek.com, September 25, 2006. <http://www.autoweek.com/apps/pbcs.dll/article?AID=/20060925/FREE/60918004/1562/nascarfeatures> (November 28, 2007).
8. Lee Spencer, "Harvick's success goes beyond the stats," *The Sporting News*, November 19, 2001. <http://findarticles.com/p/articles/mi_m1208/is_47_225/ai_80680577> (November 23, 2007).
9. Bruce Martin, "Youth Movement: Winston Cup racing turns into a proving ground for young guns," StockCarRacing.com, n.d. <http://www.stockcarracing.com/thehistoryof/32326_youth_movement_winston_cup_racing/index.html> (November 29, 2007).
10. Pete McCole, "Harvick's amazing 2001 season," AutoRacing1.com, November 27, 2001. <http://www.autoracing1.com/NASCAR/PeteM/2001/1127HarvickSeason.htm> (November 29, 2007).
11. Ibid.
12. Ibid.

13. Rick Houston, "'That's Bristol,'" scenedaily.com, September 3, 2001. http://www.scenedaily.com/stories/2001/09/03/busch_coverage2 .html (November 29, 2007).

14. Stephen Thomas, "Realized potential: Harvick dominant in Tropicana 400 victory," CNNSI.com, n.d. <http://sportsillustrated. cnn.com/motorsports/nascar_plus/news/2001/07/15/harvick_win/> (November 29, 2007).

15. Ibid.

16. Pete McCole, "Harvick's amazing 2001 season," AutoRacing1.com, November 27, 2001. <http://www.autoracing1.com/NASCAR/PeteM/2001/ 1127HarvickSeason.htm> (November 29, 2007).

17. Ibid.

CHAPTER 7. DOUBLE THREAT

1. Pete McCole, "Harvick's amazing 2001 season," AutoRacing1.com, November 27, 2001. <http://www.autoracing1.com/NASCAR/PeteM/2001/ 1127HarvickSeason.htm> (November 29, 2007).

2. Ibid.

3. "Chicagoland – Chevrolet/Team Monte Carlo Notes and Quotes," General Motors PR, July 14, 2002. <http://www.racingwest.com/ news/story.php3/4534/> (November 29, 2007).

4. Ibid.

5. Mark Aumann, "Enduring Performance: 2002 Tropicana 400," NASCAR.com, July 4, 2006. <http://superstore.nascar.com/2006/news/ headlines/cup/07/04/enduring_performance/index.html> (November 29, 2007).

6. Ibid.

7. Ibid.

8. Associated Press, "Harvick edges Burton to complete Bristol sweep," NASCAR.com, April 4, 2005. <http://www.nascar.com/2005/ news/headlines/bg/04/04/lede_bristol.ap/index.html> (November 29, 2007).

CHAPTER 8. RUNNING A TEAM

1. PA SportsTicker, Bruce Martin, "Harvicks celebrate Truck Series championship with Ron Hornaday," Yahoo.com, November 17, 2007. <http://sports.yahoo.com/nascar/news?slug=txtrucksharvickftr&prov=st&typ e=lgns> (November 23, 2007).

2. Ibid.

3. Ibid.

4. "Press Conference: DeLana and Kevin Harvick at Homestead-Miami Speedway," TruckSeries.com, November 17, 2007. <http://www.truckseries.com/cgi-script/NCTS_07/articles/000133/013321.htm> (November 23, 2007).

5. Ibid.

6. Ibid.

7. Ibid.

8. Ibid.

9. Associated Press, "Hornaday wins Truck Series title; Benson wins season finale," ESPN.com, November 16, 2007. <http://sports.espn.go.com/espn/wire?section=auto&id=3115237> (November 23, 2007).

10. Ibid.

11. "Press Conference: DeLana and Kevin Harvick at Homestead-Miami Speedway," TruckSeries.com, November 17, 2007. <http://www.truckseries.com/cgi-script/NCTS_07/articles/000133/013321.htm> (November 23, 2007).

12. Ibid.

13. Ibid.

CHAPTER 9. PUTTING THE WINS TOGETHER

1. Seth Livingstone, "Harvick holds off Stewart at Watkins Glen," USAToday.com, August 14, 2006. <http://www.usatoday.com/sports/motor/nascar/2006-08-13-watkins-glen_x.htm> (November 30, 2007).

2. Ibid.

3. Ibid.

4. "Harvick looking like he's on the right road," Chicago Sun-Times, August 10, 2007. <http://findarticles.com/p/articles/mi_qn4155/is_20070810/ai_n19477934> (November 30, 2007).

5. Ibid.

6. Seth Livingstone and Nate Ryan, "Harvick dominates at New Hampshire, takes Nextel points lead," USAToday.com, September 18, 2006. <http://www.usatoday.com/sports/motor/nascar/2006-09-17-new-hampshire_x.htm> (November 30, 2007).

7. Josh Pate, "2006 Busch Honors," NASCAR.com, November 30, 2006.<http://www.nascar.com/2006/news/headlines/bg/11/29/busch.2006.honors/index.html> (November 30, 2007).

CHAPTER 10. DAYTONA 500 CHAMPION

1. Terry Blount, "Harvick barely takes checkered at drama-filled Daytona," ESPN.com, February 18, 2007. <http://sports.espn.go.com/rpm/columns/story?seriesId=2&columnist=blount_terry&id=2770638> (November 30, 2007).

2. Ibid.

3. Associated Press, "Harvick wins Daytona 500," post-gazette.com, February 19, 2007. http://www.post-gazette.com/pg/07050/763293-132.stm (November 23, 2007).

4. Terry Blount, "Harvick barely takes checkered at drama-filled Daytona," ESPN.com, February 18, 2007. <http://sports.espn.go.com/rpm/columns/story?seriesId=2&columnist=blount_terry&id=2770638> (November 30, 2007).

5. Ibid.

6. Alan Schmadtke, "Last lap is quite a show-stopper Sunday," OrlandoSentinel.com, February 19, 2007. <http://www.orlandosentinel.com/sports/motorracing/orl-dside41907feb19,0,5383357.story> (November 30, 2007).

7. Ed Hinton, "Harvick wins Daytona 500 by 0.02 of a second," OrlandoSentinel.com, February 19, 2007. <http://www.orlandosentinel.com/sports/motorracing/orl-daytona1907feb19,0,6613682.story> (November 30, 2007).

8. Associated Press, "Harvick wins Daytona 500," post-gazette.com, February 19, 2007. http://www.post-gazette.com/pg/07050/763293-132.stm (November 23, 2007).

9. Viv Bernstein, "Amid Crashes and Controversy, Harvick Edges Martin at the Finish," NYTimes.com, February 19, 2007. <http://www.nytimes.com/2007/02/19/sports/othersports/19daytona.html> (November 23, 2007).

10. Nate Ryan, "Harvick denies Martin with dramatic victory at the Daytona 500," USAToday.com, February 20, 2007. <http://www.usatoday.com/sports/motor/nascar/2007-02-18-daytona-500_x.htm> (November 23, 2007).

11. Ibid.

12. "Press Conference: DeLana and Kevin Harvick at Homestead-Miami Speedway," TruckSeries.com, November 17, 2007. <http://www.truckseries.com/cgi-script/NCTS_07/articles/000133/013321.htm> (November 23, 2007).

13. "Harvick looking like he's on the right road," Chicago Sun-Times, August 10, 2007. <http://findarticles.com/p/articles/mi_qn4155/is_20070810/ai_n19477934> (November 30, 2007).

14. Brant James, "How a rookie helped a team cope," Sptimes.com, February 18, 2006. www.sptimes.com/2006/02/18/Sports/how_a_rookie_helped_a.shtml (November 28, 2007).

15. Raygan Swan. "Harvick, Bowyer remain in teammate Chase battle," NASCAR.com, August 4, 2008, http://www.nascar.com/2008/news/headlines/cup/08/03/kharvick.cbowyer.pocono/index.html> (November 7, 2008).

GLOSSARY

banked—A sloped racetrack, usually at a curve or corner.

caution flag (yellow flag)—Waved when drivers are required to slow down due to an accident or other hazard on the track.

chassis—The frame of a car.

checkered flag—The flag that is waved as the winner of a race crosses the start/finish line.

crew chief—The leader of the pit crew.

drafting—The aerodynamic effect that allows two or more cars traveling nose-to-tail to run faster than a car running by itself. The lead car cuts through the air, providing less resistance for the back car(s).

groove—The best route around a racetrack.

NASCAR—The National Association for Stock Car Auto Racing, the highest level of stock car racing.

pit crew—The mechanics who work as a team to make adjustments to the car, such as changing tires, during a race.

pit road—The area where pit crews service the cars, usually along the front straightaway.

pole position—The leading position at the start of a race, awarded to the fastest driver during qualifying.

qualifying—A process where cars are timed in laps on the track by themselves. The times are then compared with the fastest cars getting to start in the best positions for a race.

Rookie of the Year—The award given to the best first-year driver on the NASCAR circuit.

short track—A racetrack that is less than one mile long.

sponsor—A business that pays money to a race team, generally in exchange for advertising, such as having its logo painted on the car.

stock car—A standard type of automobile that is modified for use in racing.

superspeedway—A racetrack that is two miles or longer.

Victory Lane—The winner's circle where the winning driver parks to celebrate after the race.

INDEX